ISIAH WILLIAMS

ADOPTED

THE KEYS TO GROWING INTO YOUR KINGDOM IDENTITY.

FROM ORPHAN TO HEIR.
BREAKING THE SPIRIT OF ABANDONMENT

Published by
Keystobalance Publishing

Published by Keystobalance Publishing
United States | 2026

ISBN: 979-8-9935112-6-9

For bulk orders, speaking engagements, or inquiries, please contact: hello@reachcitychurch.org

First Edition

Disclaimer

This book is intended for personal growth, spiritual reflection, and educational purposes. It is not intended to replace professional counseling, therapy, or medical advice. Readers are encouraged to seek professional guidance where appropriate.

Dedication

To my wife,

Thank you for seeing in me what I struggled to see in myself.

You pushed me when I felt like quitting, supported me when the weight felt heavy, and reminded me that everything I needed was already within me.

This book exists because of your belief, your strength, and your unwavering love. You didn't just stand beside me—you helped pull purpose out of me.

I am forever grateful for you.

This is as much yours as it is mine.

With all my love.

Isiah Williams

Foreword

Isiah Williams is the poster child for overcoming insurmountable odds. He has the perfect blend of grit and grace.

This ability has its foundation in the immovable pillar of sonship, that upholds his belief system. Because he's secure in the blessed adoption into the family of God, the dominoes of obedient success keep falling in his favor.

This book will expose you to the reality that being an orphan spiritually is not your destination in Christ Jesus.

- Brandon Clack

Table of Contents

This Might Be You (And You Don't Even Know It)

Let me ask you something. Have you ever felt like you had to prove your place... even in rooms where you already belonged? Like no matter how much you showed up, served, or did all the right things, there was still something in the back of your mind quietly asking, "Am I really loved?" or "Do I actually belong here?" You may not say it out loud, and sometimes you may not even recognize it, but it shows up. It shows up in the way you respond to correction, the way you react when doors close, or how you feel when someone else gets chosen. It shows up in relationships—with people and even with God. Because you can call Him Father and still secretly feel like you're on your own.

This book is about something many people don't talk about, but a lot of people live with the orphan spirit. And no, this isn't about whether you had parents or not. It's about a mindset—a way of thinking and living that quietly says, "I have to figure this out on my own," "I can't fully trust love," and "I have to earn my place." The challenging part is that you can be saved, serving in church, quoting scripture, and still living internally like you don't belong.

This isn't a book written to shame you. It's written to reveal what may be hiding beneath the surface so you can finally be free. Because a lot of what people call "just how I am," "my personality," or even "being strong" can be self-protection rooted in pain, rejection, and survival. In these pages, you're going to discover how the orphan spirit develops, how it quietly shows up in everyday life, how it affects relationships, your thinking, and even your walk with God. More importantly, you're going to learn how to break free from it.

But let me say this clearly: this is not just information. This is an invitation. An invitation to stop striving, stop questioning your worth, and stop living like you've been left behind. It's an invitation to finally embrace the truth that you belong, you are chosen, and you have been adopted by the Father.

So, as you read this book, don't rush through it. Be honest. Be open. Allow these pages to challenge you and reveal things you may have never fully confronted before. Because you may recognize yourself somewhere in these chapters, and recognition is powerful. Sometimes freedom begins the moment you finally see what has been shaping you all along.

Chapter I

What Is the Orphan Spirit?

Chapter One

What Is the Orphan Spirit?

You ever met someone who looked like they had it all together on the outside—faithful at church, active in ministry, quoting all the right scriptures—yet deep down, they wrestled with the same question repeatedly, "Am I really loved?" That's the orphan spirit.

The Bible says in Romans 8:15–17: "For you have not received a spirit of slavery leading again to fear [of God's judgment], but you have received the Spirit of adoption as sons by which we cry, 'Abba! Father!'" This verse confirms that we are children of God. And if we are His children, then we are His heirs also, heirs of God and fellow heirs with Christ.

This verse gives us the blueprint. God never intended us to live as orphans. We've been adopted into His family, given the right to call Him "Abba"—Daddy, Father. And yet, many believers still live as if they've been abandoned. They call God Father, but they don't feel like His children. They know truth with their mouths, but not with their hearts.

The Inner Contradiction

The orphan spirit is not about whether you have parents, it's about a mindset, the condition of the heart. It's that gap between what you confess and what you believe.

You confess "God loves me" but wonder, "Why did they leave me?"

You sing "I am chosen" but secretly ask, "Why wasn't I picked for the job or ministry position?"

You pray "God is faithful" but fight thoughts of "What if He abandons me too?" It's a subtle mindset that creeps into church, work, and relationships. It shows up in how you view correction, how you handle closed doors, and how you process change. Change, to the orphan spirit, feels like rejection. Redirection feels like abandonment.

Why Does This Happen?

The orphan spirit is often birthed in pain—being overlooked, losing a parent, rejection in relationships, abuse, betrayal, or moments that left you feeling abandoned and unseen. It's the residue of wounds that were never fully healed, experiences that quietly shaped the way you see yourself, other people, and even God. Over time, those wounds can begin creating beliefs that say, "I'm on my own," "I can't trust people," or "I have to protect myself from being hurt again."

Jesus spoke directly to this in John 14:18 when He said, "I will not leave you as orphans; I will come to you." That statement reveals something powerful: the orphan spirit is not God's will for His children. It's an assignment rooted in lies and separation, designed to disconnect people from the reality of God's love, presence, and belonging. The enemy wants people living like they've been abandoned, while the Father continually reminds them they have been chosen and adopted.

And this is why healing matters so deeply. Because if pain is left unaddressed, it doesn't just stay a memory—it becomes a mindset. It begins shaping reactions, relationships, and expectations without people even realizing it. But Jesus didn't just come to save you from sin; He came to restore your identity. He came to heal the places where rejection convinced you that you were alone and remind you that the Father never intended for you to live like an orphan in a house where you already belong.

The Weight of Why

The orphan spirit always leaves us asking "Why?" Why wasn't I good enough? Why did they leave me? Why am I not wanted? Why does it seem like everyone else gets picked but me? Those questions may sound simple on the surface, but they carry deep pain underneath them. And if they go unanswered and unhealed, they don't just stay connected to the past, they begin bleeding into the present.

Those "why's" show up when you step into ministry. They creep in when you join a new church family, start a new relationship, or walk into unfamiliar environments. They whisper when doors close, when someone overlooks you, or when things don't go the way, you hoped they would. And it's not always loud or obvious. Sometimes it disguises itself as offense, self-protection, distance, or independence. But underneath it all is the same root belief quietly running in the background: "I don't belong."

That thought is more powerful than most people realize because once you believe it—even subconsciously—it starts shaping the way you interpret everything around you. You walk into rooms already bracing yourself for rejection. You listen to conversations through a filter of insecurity. You interpret people's actions based on past wounds instead of present truth. So when someone doesn't respond to your message, the thought becomes, "They're ignoring me." When someone corrects you, it feels like, "They don't value me." When a door closes, the orphan mindset immediately says, "I knew it… I'm not chosen."

The reality is, it's not always about what happened, it's about how the orphan mindset interprets what happened. And over time, you don't just experience rejection anymore; you start expecting it. You begin anticipating disappointment before it arrives, protecting yourself before anyone has hurt you, and pulling away before people even have the chance to come close.

But this is why healing matters so deeply. Because when the root belief changes, the interpretation begins to change too. You stop filtering life through rejection and start seeing through the lens of truth instead of pain. You begin realizing that not every closed door means you're unwanted, not every correction means you're unloved, and not every delay means you've been forgotten by God. Sometimes the greatest freedom comes from finally confronting the lie that told you didn't belong and allowing the Father to show you that you always did.

The Filter You Don't Realize You're Using

The orphan spirit creates a lens, and once that lens is in place, everything begins getting filtered through it. Love starts feeling temporary. Correction feels personal instead of helpful. Silence feels intentional, and distance immediately feels like abandonment—even when none of those things are true. The pain of past rejection begins shaping present interpretation, causing people to react not only to what is happening, but to what they fear might happen again.

That's why someone can be surrounded by people who genuinely care and still feel completely alone. They can receive affirmation and still question whether it's real. They can be chosen, included, and valued while secretly feeling overlooked and unwanted. The issue is not always what's happening around them, it's often what's happening within them. It's the internal narrative quietly influencing how every interaction, delay, correction, or relationship is being processed.

And when that lens goes unchallenged long enough, it becomes exhausting. You start carrying emotional weight into places where peace was available. You begin expecting rejection before it even arrives. Instead of resting in love, you brace for loss. Instead of receiving connection, you protect yourself from disappointment.

But healing begins when that lens is finally confronted with truth. When you start recognizing that not every silence means abandonment, not every correction means rejection, and not every difficult moment means you are unloved. The Father wants to heal the way you see, not just the way you feel. Because when your perspective changes, your relationships change, your responses change, and eventually, the way you see yourself begins to change too.

Survival Mode vs. Sonship

When the orphan spirit is active, you don't live from identity—you live from survival. You guard your heart constantly. You manage your image carefully. You stay emotionally one step ahead, so you won't get hurt again. Over time, survival becomes second nature, and what once felt like protection starts shaping the way you approach relationships, opportunities, and even God Himself.

That mindset often sounds like, "I won't open up too much," "I'll just handle it myself," or "I don't need anyone." But that's not true strength—it's self-protection. It's the result of pain teaching you that vulnerability is dangerous and dependence leads to disappointment. And while those walls may have helped you survive in one season of your life, they can quietly keep you from fully living in the next.

Because sons and daughters don't live in constant survival mode. They live safely. They don't have to fight to belong, prove their worth, or endlessly question whether they are wanted. They already know they are loved, accepted, and secure in the Father. That security changes everything. It allows them to rest instead of striving, trust instead of controlling, and connect instead of constantly protecting themselves from being hurt.

When Belief Becomes Behavior

Here's where it gets real: what you believe doesn't just stay in your mind—it eventually shows up in your life. If deep down you believe you're not wanted, you may begin withdrawing before people ever get too close. If you expect people to leave, you'll naturally keep emotional distance, so the pain won't hit as hard if they do. And if you believe love must be earned, you'll exhaust yourself trying to prove your value through performance, people-pleasing, or constantly trying to be "enough."

The dangerous part is that most people do these things without even realizing it. What's rooted in fear or self-protection often gets renamed as "being cautious," "protecting my peace," or "just how I am." But underneath those behaviors is often a heart that has learned to protect itself from rejection, disappointment, and abandonment.

And over time, those patterns can begin feeling normal. The walls, the distance, the overthinking, the emotional guarding all start feeling like part of your personality instead of a response to pain. But just because something became familiar doesn't mean it was meant to define you. Healing begins when you stop simply managing the symptoms and start confronting the beliefs underneath them.

But Here's the Truth

The orphan spirit is loud, but it is not truth. It's a learned response, a formed pattern, and a mindset built from painful moments, disappointment, rejection, and experiences that left wounds behind. Over time, those experiences can shape the way you think, react, and see yourself. But just because something was learned doesn't mean it has to remain. And just because it feels real doesn't mean it's true.

The truth is that you are not overlooked, forgotten, or outside of the family of God. You have been adopted. Chosen intentionally by the Father, not reluctantly tolerated or temporarily accepted. Your identity was never meant to be rooted in what hurt you, who rejected you, or the moments that made you question your value. Your identity is rooted in who God says you are.

And this is where the shift begins—not by pretending the pain never happened, but by confronting the beliefs that were formed because of it. Healing starts when you become honest about the patterns, the fears, and the mindsets that have quietly been shaping your life from the background. Because once you recognize the pattern, you no longer must stay trapped inside of it.

Freedom begins the moment truth becomes louder than the lies you've been rehearsing for years. The moment you stop agreeing with rejection and start agreeing with the Father. And while healing may be a process, every step toward truth is a step away from the mindset that once convinced you that you were alone.

When the Orphan Spirit Enters the Church

The orphan spirit is loud, but it is not truth. It's a learned response, a formed pattern, and a mindset built from painful moments, disappointment, rejection, and experiences that left wounds behind. Over time, those experiences can shape the way you think, react, and see yourself. But just because something was learned doesn't mean it has to remain. And just because it feels real doesn't mean it's true.

The truth is that you are not overlooked, forgotten, or outside of the family of God. You have been adopted. Chosen intentionally by the Father, not reluctantly tolerated or temporarily accepted. Your identity was never meant to be rooted in what hurt you, who rejected you, or the moments that made you question your value. Your identity is rooted in who God says you are.

And this is where the shift begins—not by pretending the pain never happened, but by confronting the beliefs that were formed because of it. Healing starts when you become honest about the patterns, the fears, and the mindsets that have quietly been shaping your life from the background. Because once you recognize the pattern, you no longer have to stay trapped inside of it.

Freedom begins the moment truth becomes louder than the lies you've been rehearsing for years. The moment you stop agreeing with rejection and start agreeing with the Father. And while healing may be a process, every step toward truth is a step away from the mindset that once convinced you that you were alone.

And the dangerous part? It can all look normal. A church can be full of activity but empty of identity. Outwardly alive, but inwardly still striving to belong.

Encountering the orphan spirit within the four walls of the church can get tricky, it's deeply covert. It often disguises itself as a quiet confidence that doesn't "need" to be seen, yet the moment recognition doesn't come or an opportunity passes by, something shifts internally. The narrative becomes: there's no place for me here. And while it may appear detached, it still feeds on attention in subtle ways.

What makes it so difficult to identify is how innocent it can seem. At its core, there may even be a genuine desire for a fresh start. But a new beginning requires honesty—and that's the challenging part. There has to be a willingness to look inward and take ownership of what's really driving those thoughts and reactions. Until that work is done, the pattern won't stay confined to one area—it will surface in every relationship and environment.

The orphan mindset resists true, connected relationships, yet still longs for them in a controlled way. It gravitates toward isolated connection where it can be understood, affirmed, and agreed with—without the depth, accountability, or vulnerability that real community requires.

And here's the reality: an orphan spirit operating in someone gifted can be especially hard to discern. It often hides behind prophetic insight, a grace for healing, a powerful preaching ability, and other visible expressions of gifting. The outward fruit can distract from the inward condition.

There is something deeply unsettling about serving a loving Father while not living from the identity of a son or daughter. This is where subtle dysfunction begins—where unhealthy dynamics can take root, where influence can become distorted, and where what we often call "church hurt" is ultimately formed.

Now here's where it gets uncomfortable and honest. Because it's one thing to talk about the orphan spirit as a concept, but it's another thing to recognize how it may be showing up in your own life. Most people don't walk around saying, "I have an orphan mindset." No, this thing is subtle. It hides in reactions, shows up in relationships, and slips into decisions without people even realizing it. And if you're not paying attention, you'll start calling it personality when it's really a pattern.

The orphan mindset doesn't just stay in your thoughts— it eventually leaks into your behavior. It shapes how you show up at work, how you connect with people, and how you respond when life doesn't go the way you expected. It can influence the way you handle correction, disappointment, relationships, opportunities, and even success. And the truth is, you can genuinely love God, faithfully serve in church, and still have areas in your life where this mindset is quietly operating beneath the surface.

So, before we go any further, I want you to slow down for a moment. Don't rush through this next part. Don't brush past it or immediately explain it away. Be honest with yourself. Because healing begins with recognition. If you can identify the pattern, you can confront it. And if you can confront it, you no longer have to stay controlled by it.

Now let's bring this out of the abstract and into real life, because freedom doesn't happen by pretending the issue isn't there. It happens when truth finally shines light on what's been quietly shaping the way you think, feel, and live all along.

Everyday Evidence

It's not just something that shows up inside church walls. The orphan spirit often reveals itself in everyday life. It can show up through the constant need to prove yourself at work because deep down, you're afraid someone will question whether you truly deserve your place. It can appear in relationships when withdrawing feels safer than risking rejection or disappointment. Sometimes it looks like refusing to ask for help because somewhere along the way you started equating need with weakness.

It can also show up in more subtle ways, like feeling relief when others fall short because their failure temporarily makes your own insecurities feel less exposed. Not because you're a bad person, but because comparison and self-protection have quietly become tied to identity and worth.

These are not just random personality traits or harmless quirks. They are often symptoms of an orphan mindset operating beneath the surface. They reveal a deeper struggle with belonging, security, and the fear of not being enough. And until those deeper beliefs are confronted, the patterns will continue repeating themselves in different areas of life.

A Heart Check

Let's be honest: have you ever looked at someone else's success and immediately felt like it was proof that you weren't enough? Have you ever questioned whether God overlooked you because someone else's prayers seemed to be answered faster than yours? Or found yourself avoiding deep accountability because vulnerability felt more threatening than safe?

If so, you've likely brushed up against the orphan spirit. Because comparison, insecurity, and the fear of being unseen don't just come from circumstances, they often come from deeper beliefs about identity, worth, and belonging. The orphan mindset quietly convinces people that someone else's blessing means there's less available for them, or that delays somehow mean they've been forgotten by God.

But this isn't about shame. It's about clarity. The more we recognize the fingerprints of the orphan spirit in our hearts, our reactions, and even our culture, the more we can surrender those areas to the Father for healing. Because hidden wounds cannot heal if they remain hidden.

And here's the reality: the orphan spirit thrives in secrecy, comparison, fear, and isolation. But once the light of truth exposes it, freedom is never far away. The moment you begin recognizing the lies you've been agreeing with is the moment you stop being controlled by them. And that recognition may be the very thing that opens the door for healing, restoration, and a deeper understanding of what it truly means to belong to the Father.

Spiritual Orphans

When you carry an orphan spirit, you live like a spiritual orphan. You may know God with your head, but your heart still lives in survival mode. You can serve faithfully and still feel unworthy. You can pray passionately and still fear rejection. You can be surrounded by people and still feel alone. That's the contradiction. Outwardly, you know Him as Father, but inwardly you feel uncovered, unprotected, and unseen. Here's the truth: the orphan spirit is a lie. The Word says in John 1:12:

"But to as many as did receive and welcome Him, He gave the right to become children of God, that is, to those who believe in His name." If you have received Christ, you are not an orphan. You are a son. You are a daughter. You are an heir!

My Story

I know this isn't just theory. I've lived it. I know what it feels like to carry the title of believer but not the assurance of sonship. I know what it's like to serve God faithfully while silently battling the thought that maybe I wasn't enough. I know the ache of abandonment, the sting of rejection, the fear of never belonging. I can vaguely remember, as a child, feeling a sense of abandonment—but not having the language to explain it. It wasn't because I wasn't loved. I was surrounded by love, covered in it. But beneath that, there was a quiet tension inside me, like I was always reaching to be seen, fighting for something I couldn't yet name.

Have you ever heard someone say, "Stop showing out"? I heard that more times than I can count. I was always trying to be the center of attention, always trying to be funny, to stand out, to pull focus without even realizing why. Looking back now, I understand what was really happening. I wasn't just trying to be seen—I was longing to be validated.

And validation, when it comes from the wrong place, can become an entry point for the orphan spirit. Pair that with unprocessed anger, and it becomes a dangerous combination. What I didn't realize then—but have come to understand now— is this: it is possible to project your emptiness onto people who never caused it. And when you do, it creates expectations they were never meant to carry. Expectations that will always go unmet.

I also know what happens when the Father speaks. I know the freedom that comes when His Spirit testifies to mine: "You are My child."

The Good News

The good news is that the orphan spirit is not permanent. It's not your identity. It's not your destiny. It's a mindset that can be broken, healed, and replaced with the truth of adoption. Through Christ, you are no longer fatherless. You are no longer left out. You are no longer defined by rejection.

You are chosen. You are seen. You are known—fully— and still deeply loved. The very places where you once felt overlooked or abandoned are the same places God desires to restore with truth, security, and belonging. This isn't about pretending the pain didn't happen; it's about allowing God to meet you in it and rewrite what it produced in you. What once shaped your reactions does not have to define your future.

There is a process to this healing. There is intentional work in renewing your mind, in confronting what you believed, and in replacing it with truth. But hear this clearly, you are not stuck. You are not too far gone. And you are not disqualified from walking in wholeness and sonship.

So don't stop here. Keep reading—because what comes next will help you not only recognize the orphan mindset but begin to break it and step fully into the identity that has always been yours.

Reflection Questions

1. What "why" questions have quietly followed you through life, and how have those questions shaped the way you see yourself, other people, or even God?

2. In what areas of your life do you find yourself living from survival instead of security? How does that show up in your relationships, work, ministry, or emotions?

3. Have there been moments where you interpreted correction, silence, distance, or closed doors through the lens of rejection? What belief may have been operating underneath that reaction?

4. What behaviors have you labeled as "just how I am" that may actually be rooted in self-protection, fear, or the orphan mindset?

5. If you truly believed you were fully loved, chosen, and adopted by the Father, what would change about the way you think, respond, rest, and connect with others?

CHAPTER II

Four Signs of the Orphan Spirit in a Believer

Chapter Two

Four Signs of the Orphan Spirit in a Believer

If the orphan spirit is real—and it is—then the next question becomes obvious: how do I know if I've been living with it? Most believers don't walk around saying, "I have an orphan spirit." It usually doesn't announce itself that clearly. Instead, it shows up quietly through patterns of thought, behavior, and even culture. It slips into relationships, service, leadership, and worship. It hides beneath the surface while influencing the way people think, respond, and connect with others.

Let me say it like this: you don't always recognize the orphan spirit when it's active—you recognize the fruit of it. You recognize the frustration, the insecurity, the overthinking, and the constant need to prove yourself, but you don't always trace those things back to the root. And that's how the cycle keeps operating. Because if something goes unnamed, it usually goes unchecked. So instead of confronting the deeper issue, people often call it stress, a bad season, or "just how things are right now," never realizing there may be an unhealed wound, an unchecked belief, or a mindset quietly shaping everything from the background.

And what makes this even more real is that the orphan spirit doesn't show up the same way for everyone. For some people, it's loud and obvious. For others, it's subtle and hidden beneath success, busyness, or performance. For some, it looks like constantly striving and overworking to feel valuable. For others, it looks like withdrawing, shutting down emotionally, or avoiding connection altogether. Some people constantly seek validation because they don't feel secure internally, while others push people away before they ever get too close. Different behaviors, same root—a fear of rejection, abandonment, or not truly belonging.

Different expressions… same root. That's why you can't always identify it just by looking at someone's life on the surface. You can be successful… and still feel insecure. You can be surrounded by people… and still feel alone. You can be affirmed… and still question your value. Because the orphan spirit doesn't care about your environment, it targets your identity.

So, the question isn't just, "Do I have this?" The better question is; "Where might this still be operating in my life?" Because if we're honest, most of us don't deal with this in one area. It shows up in layers. It might show up in your relationships… but not in your work. Or in your work…but not in your ministry.

Or in your walk with God…even while everything else looks strong. This is why awareness matters. Not so you can label yourself. Not so you can feel exposed. But so, you can finally identify what needs to be healed.

Because what you don't confront, you'll continue to carry. And what you continue to carry will eventually shape how you live, how you love, and how you see yourself. That's why these matters. Because unhealed wounds don't just disappear with time—they quietly influence your reactions, your decisions, and the way you move through life until they are finally acknowledged and confronted.

So, as we walk through these next signs, don't read them casually. Don't read them while thinking about someone else or saying, "This reminds me of them." Read it for you. Allow it to challenge you. Allow it to reveal something you may have overlooked or normalized for years. Let it bring clarity to places where confusion, frustration, or emotional exhaustion have been quietly operating beneath the surface.

Because this isn't just about gaining information. It's about recognition. And recognition is powerful because you cannot heal what you refuse to see. The moment something is exposed, it can finally be addressed. And that recognition may be the very thing God uses to begin leading you into freedom.

Now let's get specific. The good news is that God never reveals something to shame us. He reveals it to heal us. So, let's be honest about what the orphan spirit looks like, and let the Father show us the better way.

Competing and Needing to Stand Out

Spiritual orphans struggle to rest in who they are. Deep down, they often feel invisible, so they fight to be seen. That fight can show up in subtle ways—hiding weaknesses out of fear of being disqualified, viewing other people's strengths as a threat instead of a gift, or secretly feeling safer when someone else fails because comparison has become tied to identity. It can also look like constantly needing attention, recognition, or affirmation just to feel secure.

Ever been there? You receive good news but immediately wonder who's going to notice. You serve faithfully, but part of you keeps looking over your shoulder to see if anyone saw what you did. You find yourself competing for a spotlight that God never asked you to stand in because somewhere inside, validation has become connected to value.

But Paul reminds us in 1 Corinthians 12:18, "But now as things really are, God has placed and arranged the parts in the body, each one of them, just as He willed and saw fit." That means your place was intentional. Your assignment was intentional. Your value was never meant to come from outperforming everyone around you.

The truth is that sons and daughters don't compete, they are complete. When you truly know you belong, you stop measuring your worth against someone else's gift, platform, or calling. You no longer need to outshine others to feel secure because you understand that what God has for you does not require comparison to sustain it. Sons and daughters can celebrate others freely because they trust that the Father didn't overlook them when He handed out purpose.

Isolation or Independence

Deep down, the orphan spirit whispers, "You don't belong." And when that lie takes root, the natural instinct is to go through life alone. What often looks like strength on the outside is really self-protection underneath. It looks like withdrawing from people before they have the chance to leave you. It sounds like saying, "I've got this," even when you're emotionally exhausted and drowning internally. It's refusing help because somewhere along the way you started associating vulnerability with weakness.

The irony is that most people operating from an orphan mindset don't want to be alone. They deeply long for connection, safety, and genuine love, but fear keeps them isolated. Fear says, "If I depend on people, they'll disappoint me." Fear says, "If I let people in, they'll eventually leave." So instead of risking closeness, the orphan mindset convinces people to survive through independence, even when that independence is slowly draining them.

But God's answer has always been family. Ephesians 1:5 says, "He predestined and lovingly planned for us to be adopted to Himself as His own children through Jesus Christ, in accordance with the kind intention and good pleasure of His will." Adoption means belonging. It means being chosen, covered, and connected. Sons and daughters don't have to quarantine themselves in independence because they understand they were created for relationship, community, accountability, and love.

And healing often begins the moment you stop treating connection like a threat. The moment you allow yourself to be seen, supported, corrected, and cared for without immediately preparing for rejection. Because the Father never intended for His children to carry life alone. He designed family not as a burden, but as part of the healing process. And sometimes the breakthrough you've been praying for is waiting on the other side of finally letting people in.

Fear and Insecurity

The orphan spirit thrives in fear—fear of rejection, fear of failure, and fear of being exposed. And that fear often shows up in ways people don't immediately recognize. It can look like constantly needing reassurance from leaders, doubting your spiritual gifts, or questioning whether you're truly called by God. It can also show up through overprotecting your "territory" in ministry, relationships, or life because deep down you don't fully trust that God will sustain, provide, or keep what He's given you.

Maybe you've felt that tight knot in your chest when someone else gets recognized. Maybe you've experienced that low-grade panic when the affirmation you were hoping for never came. Not because you're selfish, but because insecurity quietly convinces you that your value depends on being seen, acknowledged, or validated by others. Fear has a way of making people believe there's not enough room, not enough favor, or not enough love to go around.

But Jesus addressed this directly in Matthew 10:29–31 when He said, "Are not two little sparrows sold for a copper coin? And yet not one of them falls to the ground apart from your Father's will. But even the very hairs of your head are all numbered. So do not fear; you are more valuable than many sparrows." If God cares about sparrows, He cares deeply about you. Fear is a liar, and insecurity is a thief. It steals peace, distorts identity, and keeps people living from anxiety instead of trust.

Sons and daughters live differently because they operate from security instead of fear. They know they are loved, seen, and protected by the Father. That security allows them to celebrate others without feeling threatened, trust God without constantly striving for control, and move through life without needing every moment to validate their worth.

And maybe that's the deeper invitation here—not just to stop being afraid, but to finally trust that the Father is paying attention to you. That you are not forgotten in the crowd, overlooked in the process, or competing for His affection. You are already known. Already valued. Already cared for. And when that truth settles into your heart, fear slowly begins losing its power.

Performance Orientation

The orphan spirit says, "If I perform well, I'll be loved. If I fail, I'll be rejected." So, you strive. You hustle. You work harder than everyone else, not always out of diligence, but out of desperation. You begin measuring your value by your performance, and sometimes you end up measuring others the same way. It creates a constant pressure to maintain, achieve, and prove yourself because deep down you fear what might happen if you slow down or fall short.

That mindset sounds like, "I can't rest; I might lose my place," or "If I mess this up, I'm done." It can even sound like frustration toward others: "Why can't they get it together? I worked twice as hard." But underneath all of it is fear. Fear of not being enough. Fear of losing love, acceptance, or belonging. And the truth is, performance doesn't prove love—it often hides insecurity and exhaustion.

Ephesians 1:6 reminds us that we are already "accepted in the Beloved." That means approval is not something you have to earn through constant effort or perfection. Sons and daughters live from love, not for it. They work from a place of identity, not desperation. They understand that rest is not weakness and that their value is not hanging on their latest success or failure.

Before you become defensive, hear this clearly: these signs are not here to condemn you. They are here to reveal where healing is needed. Maybe you recognize competition in your heart, isolation when you're hurt, insecurity even in places where you know you're called, or the constant drive to push yourself to exhaustion hoping it will finally make you feel worthy. If any of that resonates with you, don't run from it. Let it become a mirror instead of a hammer. Let it expose what has been quietly operating beneath the surface so healing can begin.

God's Spirit of adoption is here to replace striving with rest, fear with peace, isolation with belonging, and competition with identity. The orphan spirit may manifest in different ways, but the root is always the same: a heart that doubts its place in the Father's house. But the truth has never changed—you already belong. You were never fighting for a place at the table; you were fighting to believe the seat was already yours.

And maybe that's the freedom God has been trying to lead you into all along. Not a life of endless performance, pressure, and proving, but a life rooted in identity. A life where you no longer have to exhaust yourself trying to earn what the Father has already given freely through love. Because once you truly understand you are a son or daughter, everything changes. You stop living like someone trying to survive rejection and start living like someone who finally knows they are home.

Reflection Questions

1. Which of the four signs resonated with you the most, and why do you think that area impacts you so deeply? As you reflect, consider how it may be affecting your relationships, your thinking, or the way you respond to God and others.

2. Can you recall a specific time when competition, isolation, fear, or performance influenced your decisions or reactions? Looking back now, what belief or insecurity may have been operating underneath that moment?

3. In what ways has the orphan mindset shaped your church experience, leadership, or involvement in ministry? Have there been moments where rejection, comparison, fear, or the need to prove yourself affected how you connected with people or served?

4. What would it look like for you to fully respond to the Father's invitation in these areas of your life? What would change if you truly believed you were already loved, chosen, accepted, and secure in Him?

CHAPTER III

Self-Sabotage

Chapter Three

Self-Sabotage

L et's talk about something most people don't like to admit. Not out loud, anyway. Because it's easier to point at what didn't work than to look at what we may have walked away from. It's easier to say, "That wasn't for me," than to honestly ask, "Did I leave too soon?"

If you're honest, there have probably been moments in your life where something good showed up—an opportunity, a relationship, or a place of growth. And instead of leaning in, you pulled back. Not always in an obvious way. Sometimes it looked like hesitation. Sometimes it looked like overthinking. Sometimes it looked like "waiting on the right time." But deep down, something in you couldn't fully trust it, fully receive it, or fully rest in it. So you created distance. You slowed down. You questioned everything. And eventually, you walked away. Not because it wasn't good, but because something inside of you didn't feel safe keeping it.

That's a hard truth, but it's a real one. Because not everything we lose was taken from us. Some things we let go of. Some things we pushed away. Some things we sabotaged before they ever had the chance to become what they were meant to be. And if we're not careful, we'll keep repeating those patterns while convincing ourselves it's wisdom, discernment, or "protecting our peace," when in reality it's fear disguising itself as self-protection. It's the orphan mindset trying to stay in control because control feels safer than vulnerability.

So, before you read the rest of this chapter, I want you to do something simple, but honest. Think about the last thing in your life that had real potential. Did it truly fall apart…or did you slowly pull away from it? Because healing begins the moment we stop blaming everything outside of us and become willing to confront what fear has been teaching us to avoid. Now let's talk about it.

How the Orphan Spirit Keeps You From Good Things

Have you ever left something good before it had the chance to leave you? That's self-sabotage.

Most people don't realize they're doing it until it's over. They ghost a good thing. They walk away from a real opportunity. They push away the people who are trying to love them.

Self-sabotage is one of the orphan spirit's favorite defense mechanisms. It dresses up as "wisdom." It calls itself "being realistic." But it's fear.

It whispers, "Don't get your hopes up." It warns, "Play it safe." It insists, "They'll probably leave anyway."

Scripture makes this plain in Proverbs 23:7: "For as a man thinks in his heart, so is he." What lives internally will always find a way to express itself externally. In other words, where the mind goes, life will follow.

You can say all the right things and even convince yourself that you're free from this, but over time, your patterns will tell the truth. Your reactions, your relationships, your responses to consistency, they will reveal what you truly believe deep down.

Suspicious of Peace

Have you ever found yourself asking, "What's the catch?" when something finally starts going right? That's the orphan spirit talking. It's that internal alarm system that goes off the moment peace shows up—like peace is suspicious. You can't relax. You can't rest. You're stuck scanning the horizon, waiting for something to fall apart. Why? Because the orphan spirit doesn't know how to trust consistency. It's lived too long in instability. Toxic environments feel more comfortable than healthy ones. Dysfunction feels safer than healing. When something solid shows up—God's presence, a healthy church, a faithful mentor, or a real opportunity it can feel off. Blessings feel booby-trapped. Stability feels like a setup. Instead of leaning in, you pull back.

Control Is a False Comfort

Let's talk about control. Why is control so attractive when you're wounded? Because control feels like protection. The orphan spirit thrives on the illusion that if you can manage everything, your relationships, your emotions, your opportunities, you won't get hurt.

But here's the truth: control is a lie. It promises peace but delivers anxiety. It wears you out. You can't enjoy blessings because you're too busy guarding them. And when you can't control something fully, you'd rather kill it than risk losing it.

That's why people walk away from doors God opened. That's why we avoid applying for things we want. That's why some believers ghost mentors, leave churches, or run from accountability. Deep down, we'd rather sabotage a gift than risk being rejected while holding it.

The Saul Syndrome

Let's put some Bible on it. Saul, Israel's first king, was anointed, chosen, and positioned. But he carried big orphan's energy. In 1 Samuel 13, when pressure came, Saul panicked. He couldn't wait for Samuel to arrive to offer the sacrifice, so he did it himself, afraid the people would leave him.

In 1 Samuel 15, God told him to destroy the Amalekites, but Saul disobeyed. He kept the best livestock and spared the king because he wanted the people's approval more than God's instruction.

Fear was Saul's fuel. And when fear drives you, sabotage follows. He started well, but he couldn't finish because he never got healed. He was operating as a king with the heart of an orphan. And when your healing doesn't match your elevation, your crown becomes a curse.

Two Forms of Sabotage

Self-sabotage tends to show up in two major ways: emotionally and spiritually. Emotional sabotage can look like blowing up relationships before people get too close, walking away from accountability when conversations become uncomfortable, avoiding conflict instead of working through it, or hiding behind humor whenever things start getting too deep or too real. Spiritual sabotage often shows up through ignoring God's voice, resisting correction, delaying what He asked you to do, or leaving places of growth and community right before breakthrough begins to happen.

The actions may look different on the surface, but the root is often the same: fear of abandonment. Somewhere along the way, the orphan mindset learned that it was safer to leave first, shut down first, or disconnect first rather than risk disappointment, rejection, or vulnerability. So instead of trusting love, favor, or growth, self-sabotage steps in to protect the wound.

But sonship changes the way you respond. Sons don't run from correction because they understand correction is connected to love, not rejection. Sons don't flinch when favor shows up because they no longer believe blessings are temporary or undeserved. Sons don't fear being chosen because they know their identity is secure in the Father. Security allows them to stay, grow, heal, and trust even when it feels unfamiliar.

And maybe that's the real battle for many people—not whether God is willing to bless them, but whether they feel safe enough to remain in what He's building. Because the orphan spirit survives by keeping people disconnected, guarded, and constantly preparing for loss. But the Father is teaching His sons and daughters how to stop running. How to remain. How to trust that what He is building in their life does not have to be destroyed by fear.

Real-Life Signs You Might Be Self-Sabotaging

Let's make it plain. Here are some signs you may be sabotaging the very blessings God is trying to give you. You procrastinate on opportunities you've been praying for because deep down you're afraid of failing, being seen, or finally stepping into responsibility. You ghost mentors, leaders, or people who challenge you to grow because growth feels uncomfortable and accountability exposes the areas you've learned to hide.

You push away healthy people because their love feels unfamiliar. Chaos feels normal, but consistency feels suspicious. You criticize environments that confront your dysfunction because it's easier to protect your patterns than face the healing process. You avoid vulnerability even when it's safe because somewhere along the way you learned that opening up could lead to rejection or disappointment. And sometimes you tell yourself, "I'm protecting my peace," when in reality, you're running. Running from intimacy. Running from healing. Running from the very thing God may be using to transform your life.

Sound familiar? Because this is how the orphan mindset quietly operates. It doesn't always look dramatic. Sometimes it looks like hesitation, distance, avoidance, or constantly finding reasons not to trust what God is trying to place in front of you.

The Lie of Isolation

One of the biggest lies the orphan spirit tells is, "You're better off alone." But isolation isn't safety—it's slow spiritual death. Healing happens in community. Growth happens in accountability. Stability is built in a spiritual family.

The orphan spirit convinces you that depending on others is a weakness. But the truth is that independence without intimacy is insecurity in disguise.

From Surviving to Standing

If self-sabotage is survival mode, then sonship is standing mode. Sons and daughters don't flinch when favor shows up—they lean into it. They no longer feel the need to push away opportunities, love, or healthy relationships out of fear that it will all disappear anyway. Sons and daughters also don't ghost purpose when things become uncomfortable or challenging. They show up, even when insecurity tries to convince them to run. And they don't run from correction either. They welcome it because they understand that correction is not rejection—it's proof of love, growth, and belonging.

The orphan spirit taught you to protect yourself at all costs, but sonship teaches you to trust the Father, even when trust feels risky. It teaches you that not every open door is a trap, not every relationship is temporary, and not every blessing is going to be taken away from you. Sonship begins healing the part of you that constantly expects disappointment and reminds you that you no longer have to live in survival mode.

Self-sabotage is not the ending of your story. It's simply a strategy the orphan spirit has used to keep you stuck, isolated, and afraid of becoming everything God created you to be. But God's invitation is clear: you don't have to destroy what He's trying to bless. You don't have to tear down what He's trying to build in your life. The same hands that are healing you are also trying to establish you.

And maybe that's the shift happening right now. Maybe for the first time, you're recognizing that the battle was never just about behavior—it was about identity. Because when someone believes they are abandoned, they will eventually sabotage the very things they've been praying for. But when someone begins seeing themselves as loved, chosen, and secure in the Father, they stop resisting the good things God is bringing into their life.

It's time to stop sabotaging your future. There's a son in you. There's a daughter in you. And they're worth saving. They're worth healing. They're worth fighting for. And the beautiful part is this: God has never stopped fighting for them either.

Reflection Questions

1. Can you identify a time in your life when you pulled away from something good—a relationship, opportunity, community, or calling—because fear, insecurity, or rejection made it feel safer to leave than stay? Looking back now, what do you think you were really protecting yourself from?

2. What areas of your life do you find yourself trying to over-control instead of fully trusting and surrendering them to God? How has that need for control affected your peace, relationships, or ability to rest?

3. Is there a person, conversation, or environment you've been avoiding because it challenges you to grow, heal, or confront truth about yourself? What emotions or fears come up when you think about leaning into that growth instead of resisting it?

4. What would it look like for you to stop sabotaging what God is building in your life and begin standing firmly in your identity as a son or daughter? What changes would need to happen in your thinking, your choices, or your responses moving forward?

CHAPTER IV

The Reflection — The Transforming of the Mind

Chapter Four

The Reflection — The Transforming of the Mind

Let's talk about the part nobody sees. Not your actions. Not your habits. Not even your behavior. It's what you're thinking. Because you can change what you do and still struggle with what you believe. You can show up differently on the outside and still feel the same on the inside—still insecure, still questioning, still wondering if you're enough. And that's the frustration for a lot of people. You've prayed. You've tried. You've committed to doing better. Yet somehow, despite all the effort, the internal battle still feels the same because the thoughts underneath the behavior were never fully addressed.

That's why so many people end up exhausted. They're fighting external habits while internal beliefs continue running unchecked. They've learned how to manage appearances, but not how to confront the thoughts quietly shaping their identity. So even when progress is happening, it can still feel like something is missing. Because true transformation doesn't happen when behavior changes alone. It happens when the mind finally begins to agree with the truth instead of the lies it's been rehearsing for years.

But somehow…you keep ending up in the same place mentally. Same thoughts. Same fears. Same internal conversations.

Why? Because behavior isn't the root. Belief is. You don't live based on what you know… you live based on what you believe. And if your beliefs haven't been challenged, then they've been running your life.

Quietly.

That's why you can hear the truth on Sunday and still struggle by Monday. That's why you can read scripture and still feel disconnected from it.

That's why you can say, "God loves me," and still question it when life doesn't go your way. Because somewhere along the way, something else was written into your thinking. And until that gets addressed, nothing else will fully change.

You Can't Think Like an Orphan and Live Like a Son.

Let's be real. You can't keep thinking like an orphan and expect to live like a son. There's a shift that must happen—not just in how you act, but in how you think.

Because most of us aren't struggling with behavior, we're struggling with belief. You can fix your schedule. You can join a church. You can even serve faithfully and still be tormented by the same lies in your head if your mind hasn't been renewed.

The Battle You Can't See

Most people think the real battle is external, situations, people, opportunities, doors opening and closing. But the real battle? It's internal.

It's the conversation happening in your mind. It's the thoughts you don't say out loud. The ones that sound like:

- "I'm not ready."
- "I'm going to mess this up."

- "They're going to leave eventually."
- "I don't belong here."

And the dangerous part is…you've heard those thoughts so many times they don't feel like lies anymore.

They feel like the truth, so you stop questioning them. You start agreeing with them. And before you know it… you begin living from them. That's how strongholds are formed—not overnight, but over time through repeated thoughts, reinforced beliefs, and lies left unchallenged.

And this is where the orphan mindset really takes root. Because it doesn't just affect how you feel—it affects how you interpret everything. You don't just experience life, you filter it through rejection, through fear, and through insecurity. So even love can feel unsafe. Correction can feel like abandonment. Silence can feel personal. You begin reacting to people, situations, and even God based on wounds you never fully healed from. And over time, that lens becomes so normal, you stop realizing you're seeing life through pain instead of truth.

So even when something good happens…you question it. Even when someone shows up for you…you doubt it. Even when God is moving…you hesitate to trust it. Not because He's not faithful.

But because your thinking hasn't caught up to the truth yet. And if we're being honest, this is where a lot of believers get stuck.

Saved, but still struggling. Free, but still thinking like they're bound. Chosen, but still feeling overlooked. Because you can't walk in freedom with a mindset that's still in bondage. That's why this chapter matters. Not just so you can learn something, but so you can unlearn what's been holding you back. Because until your mind shifts, your life won't.

The Power of Belief

Let's start here. What lies have you lived by that felt like truth? Maybe it sounded like, "If I don't perform, I'm not valuable," or "Love always leaves." Maybe somewhere along the way you started believing, "I have to prove myself," "I'm too much," or "I'm not enough." These lies don't usually scream, they whisper. They settle quietly into your thinking and begin shaping how you walk into a room, how you receive corrections, and how you interpret silence. And before you know it, you're no longer responding from truth, you're reacting to life based on wounds instead of the Word.

Saved, But Still Struggling

You can be saved and still not secure. That's that weird in-between place—you believe in Jesus, but you're afraid He might change His mind about you. You pray, but you still serve from a place of fear. You belong, but you don't feel at home.

This is what Paul meant when he wrote:

Romans 12:2 – "Be transformed by the renewing of your mind."

Behavior doesn't change until belief does. You won't stop sabotaging until you believe you're worthy of love. You won't rest until you believe you're already accepted. Sons and daughters live from approval, not for it.

What Renewal Looks Like

Renewal isn't a one-time moment. It's daily. It's choosing truth when your feelings lie. It's catching toxic thoughts in the middle of the cycle and stopping long enough to ask, "Where did that come from?" It's becoming aware of the patterns that have been running quietly in the background for years and finally refusing to let them lead your life anymore.

It's replacing shame with the Father's voice. It's journaling your thoughts and lining them up with scripture instead of emotion. It's interrupting the loop of rejection and speaking truth over yourself until your mind begins to believe it: "I am chosen. "I am loved." I am called." This isn't about memorizing the right answers, it's about allowing God to rewrite the script you've been living by.

Lies vs. Truth

Here's a few to get you started:

The Lie	The Truth
I have to earn love.	I am loved *because I am.*
I'll always be overlooked.	I am seen and *known by God.*
I'm not good enough.	His grace is *sufficient.*
I have to *hold it all.*	It is *safe to let God carry this.*
God is *disappointed in me.*	He delights in me.

Your turn: **What lies have you believed that you need to replace?**

From Performing to Resting

There's a difference between performing for love and resting in it. Performance is exhausting because it keeps you striving, anxious, and constantly wondering if you've done enough to be accepted. It teaches you to hide your weaknesses, cover your flaws, and live afraid that if people see the real you, they might walk away. But resting in love produces peace. It allows you to stop pretending and trust that grace covers every part of you—not just the polished parts. Sons don't live trying to earn what the Father has already given them. They abide.

Reflection Questions

1. What lies or beliefs have quietly shaped the way you see yourself, others, or God more than you realized? As you reflect, ask yourself where those beliefs may have originally come from and how they've been influencing your decisions, relationships, or sense of worth.

2. In what areas of your life are you still performing for love, approval, or acceptance instead of resting in the security of being fully loved by the Father? How has striving affected your peace, your identity, or the way you relate to God?

3. When it comes to your identity, are you allowing scripture to define who you are, or are past wounds, rejection, and painful experiences speaking louder than truth? What thoughts or reactions reveal which voice you've been agreeing with the most?

4. What would it practically look like for you to live from a renewed mind this week? What thoughts need to be challenged, what truths need to be repeated, and what patterns may need to change so your life begins aligning more with who God says you are?

CHAPTER V

The Father's Invitation

Chapter Five

The Father's Invitation

Let me ask you something. What comes to mind when you hear the word, Father? Not the church's answer. Not the "right" answer. Your real answer. Because for some people, that word brings comfort. For others, it brings confusion. And for some... it brings pain.

It brings back memories they've tried to move past. Disappointment from promises that were never kept. The ache of absence where love and protection should have been. Silence during moments they needed guidance, reassurance, or simply someone to stay. And whether people realize it or not, those experiences often shape the way they see God. Because when the earthly version of "father" was connected to hurt, distance, or inconsistency, it can become difficult to trust the heart of a Heavenly Father who says He will never leave.

And whether you realize it or not...that experience shapes how you see God. You can hear that God is loving, but still feel distant from Him. You can know He's present but still feel like you're on your own. You can call Him Father and still struggle to trust Him like one.

Why? Because the orphan spirit doesn't just affect how you see yourself, it affects how you see Him. And if your view of God is filtered through pain, through absence, through disappointment, then His invitation can feel unfamiliar. Even uncomfortable. Because love that stays is hard to receive when all you've known is love that leaves.

But here's the truth: God has never invited you into a relationship based on performance. He has never said, "Get it together, then come to Me," or "Be perfect before you can belong." His invitation has always been the same: come home. God's invitation is not like man's. It's not inconsistent, conditional, or based on how well you perform. And it is never revoked. His love is a covenant, not a temporary arrangement.

Think of it this way: the light will always be on. I remember growing up as a teenager, going out with friends, and no matter how late I came home past curfew, I knew the light would still be on and there would always be a home for me to return to. That sense of security mattered more than I realized at the time. But many believers who struggle with the orphan mindset quietly assume that when they fail, make mistakes, or fall short, they've somehow lost their place with God—that the door is closed and they've been locked out. But that is not the heart of the Father.

Luke 15 paints a completely different picture. The father didn't run toward the prodigal son to shame him, lecture him, or remind him of everything he did wrong. He ran to restore him. There was no probation period, no test to earn his way back into the family. The father responded with a robe, a ring, and a celebration because sonship had never been removed, even during the son's rebellion.

So here's a question I really want you to sit with: what else does God have to do to prove that He loves you and that you will always have a home with Him? Luke 15:31 says, "Son, thou art ever with me, and all that I have is thine." The Holy Spirit is not just a Comforter—He is the Spirit of adoption (Romans 8:15). His presence is evidence that you belong to the Father.

Natural fathers may leave, disappoint, or fall short. Spiritual fathers can guide, teach, and point the way, but they are still human. God the Father, however, is the ultimate embrace—constant, safe, faithful, and healing. He is the Father who does not abandon, reject, or change His mind about His children. And when that truth finally settles into your heart, it changes the way you approach God, yourself, and every relationship connected to belonging.

Sometimes, our mistrust of God stems from broken DNA—generational patterns of rejection, abandonment, or emotional neglect. But the blood of Jesus gives us new spiritual DNA. And in it is healing, inheritance, and home.

Believe it or not, we often put unmet expectations and disappointment from our physical fathers on our spiritual fathers. That makes it hard for the spiritual father to fully do all that he needs to do and prohibits him from producing the fruit he needs in your life because you expect him to be your actual father. And when he misses the mark, he now must pay for past offenses that don't even belong to him. He starts at a disadvantage. For many people, this is where the struggle is. Not understanding the invitation, but receiving it.

Because it's one thing to hear about God as Father, it's another thing to experience Him that way. And if we're honest, some of us have spent more time relating to God as Judge, authority, or distant provider rather than Father. So instead of resting, we strive. Instead of receiving, we perform. Instead of coming close, we keep our distance. We pray but still feel guarded. We worship but still feel unsure if we're fully accepted. Deep down, many people are still approaching God through the lens of survival instead of sonship.

But what if you could hear His heart clearly? Not filtered through pain. Not shaped by past experiences or influenced by what you've been through. Just Him, speaking directly to you— not to correct you, not to shame you, and not to remind you of where you've fallen short, but to remind you of who you are. To remind you that you are loved, seen, chosen, and wanted. So, before you read this next part, take a moment. Slow down. Let your guard down and allow yourself to receive. Because these aren't just words on a page. This is an invitation to encounter the Father in a way that heals the places performance never could.

A Letter from the Father

My Beloved Child,

I saw you long before the world ever had a name for you. Before rejection touched your story. Before the ones who should've stayed walked away. Before the silence in the room became louder than the love you needed—I saw you.

You've wondered if you are wanted. You've asked if you're enough. You've questioned whether My promises apply to you or just everyone else. I've heard the whispers in your mind and the shouts in your soul that say, "I'm not chosen. I'm not enough. No one cares..." But I need you to hear Me now, not just with your ears, but with your heart:

You are Mine.

You are not abandoned. You are not forgotten.

You were never a mistake.

I didn't choose you reluctantly—I chose you on purpose. I've walked with you through every tear you didn't know how to explain. I've carried you when you didn't have the strength to stand. And I've waited—not impatiently but faithfully— for the day you'd stop running from Me, but to Me, and realize I never left.

You don't have to strive anymore.

You don't have to perform for My affection. I'm not like the ones who left.

I'm not ashamed of your wounds.

I am so proud of you. The way you have navigated traumas and storms, the way you have found the strength to keep going even when you have every reason to stop. I realized that there were people who came in My name and left you with a ton of scars. That wasn't Me, but I know you blamed Me—and that's okay.

Come home—not just with your body, but with your heart. Let Me be the Father you've longed for. The One who stays. The One who heals. The One who calls you son, daughter, not because you earned it—but because I made you family.

My arms are still open.

The table still has your name on it. The light is still on.

And I still delight in you.

Love always, Your Father

The orphan spirit wants you to believe you're unwanted, but the Father's invitation proves you're desired. And the moment you say yes, everything changes. Take a moment and sit with that. Don't rush past it. Don't analyze it. Just sit with it. Because for some of you, that may be the first time you've ever allowed yourself to hear God like that—not distant, not disappointed, and not waiting for you to finally get it right, but present, patient, and pursuing you even in the middle of your struggle.

The orphan spirit whispers that you have to earn your way back, that you've messed up too much, and that you no longer belong here. It convinces people to live as if love has conditions and acceptance has limits. But the Father's invitation speaks differently. It reminds you that you were never abandoned, never forgotten, and never too far gone. While the orphan mindset pushes you to run, hide, and strive, the Father continues to call you closer, reminding you that you never left His heart.

And that's the difference. You don't come back as a servant. You don't come back on probation. You don't come back trying to prove anything. You come back as a son. As a daughter. As someone who already belongs. The door was never locked. The light was never turned off. The invitation was never withdrawn. The only question left is this:

Will you receive it? Because the moment you do, everything changes. Not because your circumstances shift overnight, but because your identity does.

And when you finally see yourself the way the Father sees you…You stop striving. You stop questioning. You stop running. And you start living like you belong

Reflection Questions

1. Do you truly believe you belong at the Father's table, or are there still areas in your heart that feel like you have to earn your place? What thoughts, fears, or past experiences make it difficult for you to fully receive that you are already chosen and accepted?

2. Which part of the Father's invitation do you feel most drawn to right now—acceptance, belonging, security, grace, or rest? Why do you think that particular area speaks so deeply to where you currently are in your journey?

3. What has made it difficult for you to receive God as Father instead of only relating to Him as Lord, Judge, or authority? Are there past wounds, disappointments, or beliefs that have affected the way you experience His love and closeness?

CHAPTER VI

The Seat at the Table

Chapter Six

The Seat at the Table

Before we go any further, I want you to think about something. Where did you learn who you are? Not just what people told you, but what you picked up along the way. Because identity isn't just taught—it's formed. It's shaped in moments, in experiences, in what was said, and sometimes in what was never said at all. Some people learned who they were through affirmation and consistency. Others learned through absence, silence, rejection, and trying to figure life out on their own.

And if we're honest, a lot of what we believe about ourselves today didn't come from truth. It came from interpretation. Interpretation of who stayed and who left. Who showed up and who didn't. Over time, those moments started building a narrative deep within us: "This is who I am. This is what I can expect. This is how life works for me." And the dangerous part is that once that narrative is formed, you begin living from it without even realizing it. Your reactions, your relationships, your fears, and even the way you see God can start flowing from conclusions you formed in pain rather than truth.

And once those beliefs take root, they begin shaping more than your thoughts—they start shaping your identity. You begin expecting rejection before it happens. You brace yourself for disappointment. You question love, doubt your value, and struggle to trust people who genuinely care about you. Not because you want to, but because your mind has been trained to protect you from getting hurt again.

The problem is that survival-based thinking may help you cope for a season, but it was never meant to define your life. What protected you in one chapter can quietly imprison you in the next. And many people are still reacting from old wounds while calling it wisdom, discernment, or "just being careful." But underneath it all is often a heart that learned how to survive without ever truly feeling safe.

This is why healing requires more than behavior change. It requires confronting the story you've been telling yourself about who you are. Because if the narrative is never challenged, the cycle continues. But when truth enters the picture, something begins to shift. You start realizing that your experiences may have influenced you, but they do not have the final authority over your identity. God does. And He is not building your identity from your wounds, your failures, or who walked away. He's building it from who He says you are.

You walk into rooms already decided. You approach relationships already guarded. You respond to opportunities already unsure. Not because it's true, but because it's familiar. And for many people, that internal narrative sounds like, "You're on your own," "You have to figure this out," and "No one is coming." Those thoughts don't just appear out of nowhere— they are the voice of the orphan mindset, shaped through disappointment, survival, and years of trying to protect yourself from being hurt again.

But here's the truth this chapter is about to confront: that voice may have shaped you, but it does not define you. At some point, you have to decide whether you're going to keep living from what happened to you or start living from who God says you are. Because healing begins when you stop building your identity around pain and start allowing truth to speak louder than your past. And sometimes that shift doesn't begin with a lesson or a breakthrough moment. Sometimes it starts with simple honesty—finally being willing to acknowledge where you've been, what shaped you, and how those experiences have been influencing the way you see yourself all along.

I can remember growing up as a child, my father was incarcerated when I was just three years old. Things became difficult for me as a growing boy. I often say, "A father out of the home is like not having a mirror in the house; you don't know what you look like."

Without that mirror, I struggled to understand who I was. As I got older, it became harder to navigate relationships, especially with authority figures. I didn't realize it at the time, but I was avoiding authority because I subconsciously believed it had failed me.

A missing father left me with a silent message: You're on your own. But something shifted when I made the choice to forgive him. It wasn't easy, and it didn't happen overnight. Forgiveness forced me to confront pain I had buried for years, but when I forgave my father, my heart began to open—not just toward him, but toward others. It was freeing. I realized something important: it wasn't my fault that my dad wasn't there, but it was my responsibility to choose how I responded to the people who were genuinely trying their best to love and support me.

Forgiveness didn't just heal a relationship. It healed something inside of me. It broke the agreement I had unknowingly made with rejection and allowed me to stop viewing life through the lens of abandonment. For so long, I carried the weight of feeling unwanted without realizing how deeply it was affecting the way I trusted, loved, and connected with people. But forgiveness made room in my heart to believe something different—that I am, and always have been, a son.

And sometimes that's what healing really looks like. Not pretending the pain never happened but refusing to let it continue defining your identity. Because when you begin releasing what hurt you, you also begin making room for truth. You stop living like someone abandoned and start seeing yourself the way the Father sees you—wanted, chosen, and deeply loved.

Living From Love, Not For It

By now, you've seen the orphan spirit for what it is—its lies, its sabotage, these exhausting patterns. You've also caught a glimpse of the Father's heart—the invitation to belong, to be secure, to be adopted.

But here's the real turning point: sonship and daughter ship aren't just something you learn. It's something you live. It's one thing to know the truth. It's another way to let it transform how you walk, speak, and see yourself.

Because when sonship truly becomes real to you, it changes the way you move through life. You stop living from fear and start living from identity. You no longer need to prove your worth, compete for acceptance, or constantly question whether you belong. There's a confidence that comes from knowing who your Father is and who you are because of Him. Not pride. Not arrogance. Just security. The kind of security that allows you to rest, trust, and stop striving to earn what has already been freely given.

And this is where transformation begins to show up in everyday life. You start responding differently to rejection because it no longer defines you. You stop chasing validation from people because your value is no longer dependent on their approval. You begin loving from a full place instead of an empty one. The orphan mindset taught you to survive, but sonship teaches you how to live. It teaches you that you are not abandoned, forgotten, or overlooked by God. You are His. And once that truth moves from your head into your heart, it changes everything.

No Longer Slaves

Paul said it plainly in Galatians 4:7:

"So, you are no longer a slave, but God's child; and since you are His child, God has made you also an heir."

That's your reality now: You are no longer an outsider. No longer a servant or a slave. You are a child of God. And children don't beg for crumbs when they already have a seat at the table.

The orphan spirit drives you to earn what's already been freely given. Sonship and daughter-ship remind you it's already yours.

Living Like You Belong

Embracing your place as a son or daughter doesn't mean you'll never feel fear again, and it doesn't mean the orphan spirit won't still try to knock on your door. But it does mean you no longer have to answer. When fear whispers, "You're not enough," sons and daughters respond from truth instead of insecurity: "I am chosen and loved." When shame tries to convince you that you don't belong, you remember that the Father adopted you and made a place for you long before you ever earned it. And when comparison begins creeping into your thoughts, you no longer have to compete for value because your identity is already secure in Him.

Sons and daughters walk differently. They serve from joy instead of pressure. They love without constantly fearing rejection or abandonment. They don't spend their lives striving to prove themselves because they already know who they belong to. Even when life becomes difficult, they stay grounded because they understand they are covered, claimed, and called. And that kind of security changes the way you carry yourself, the way you love others, and the way you move through the world.

Heirs With Christ

Romans 8:17 says:
"If we are children, then we are heirs—heirs of God
and co-heirs with Christ, if indeed we share in His
sufferings so that we may also share in His glory."

This scripture is about more than just belonging—it's about inheritance. It's about understanding that everything connected to Jesus is now connected to you through sonship and daughtership. His peace becomes available to you in the middle of chaos. His authority becomes your confidence when fear tries to overwhelm you. His joy becomes your strength when life feels heavy, and His future becomes your hope when uncertainty tries to cloud your vision. When darkness presses in, you don't have to live defeated because you now walk in His light. And when the enemy tries accusing you with your past, your failures, or your mistakes, you stand firmly in His righteousness instead of your own.

You don't just get to sit at the table—you carry the family name. That means your identity is no longer rooted in rejection, abandonment, fear, or striving. It's rooted in the Father. Sons and daughters don't approach life begging for scraps of acceptance because they already know what belongs to them through relationship. They understand that inheritance is not earned through performance; it is received through belonging.

And maybe that's the shift many people need to make. Stop living like someone trying to convince God to let you stay and start living like someone who already belongs in the house. Because an orphan mindset constantly fears losing what sonship already secured. But when you truly understand who you are in the Father, you stop approaching life from lack, fear, and insecurity. You begin living from identity, authority, and peace.

The Father did not adopt you just so you could survive spiritually. He adopted you so you could live fully as His child. Covered by His love. Secure in His promises. Confident in His presence. And once that truth settles into your heart, it changes the way you pray, the way you walk, and the way you face every battle in front of you.

A Father's Embrace

Picture this: God's arms wrapping around you, not because you performed well, but simply because you're His. No striving. No pretending. No performance. Just love. The kind of love that doesn't fluctuate with your mistakes, your emotions, or your ability to "get it right." You don't have to earn His approval because you already have it. You don't have to chase His presence because He already promised, "I will never leave you nor forsake you" (Hebrews 13:5).

Sonship and daughter-ship are more than a concept—they are an embrace. It's the deep, unshakable reality that you are no longer homeless; you are home. No longer wandering through life trying to find where you belong, searching for validation in people, performance, or success. In the Father, you have been fully seen, fully known, and still fully loved.

And maybe that's what your heart has been searching for all along. Not another achievement. Not more recognition. Not another way to prove your worth. But rest. The kind of rest that comes from finally realizing you don't have to fight for a place that has already been prepared for you. Because when you truly understand that you belong to the Father, you stop living like someone trying to survive and start living like someone who has finally come home.

Practical Ways to Live as Sons and Daughters

Here's how this truth becomes your daily rhythm: you begin praying like a child instead of someone trying to impress God. You stop approaching Him with distance and start calling Him Abba, allowing your relationship with Him to become personal, honest, and real. You also begin letting go of the constant striving. No more exhausting attempts to earn love that has already been freely given to you through the Father.

You stay connected to healthy communities because healing rarely happens in isolation. The orphan mindset wants people disconnected, guarded, and hidden, but growth often happens when you allow yourself to be seen, supported, and challenged by others who genuinely care. You also start receiving corrections differently. Instead of viewing it as rejection or proof that you've failed, you begin recognizing that discipline is love. It's the Father shaping you, not abandoning you.

And as this truth becomes rooted deeper in your heart, you begin speaking identity over yourself on purpose. You stop repeating the language of fear, shame, and abandonment and start declaring truth instead: "I am not abandoned. I am a child of God." At first it may feel unfamiliar, but over time your mind begins aligning with what heaven has been saying about you all along. Because transformation happens when truth is repeated enough to become the new foundation you live from.

There will still be moments when old thoughts try to return. Days when insecurity whispers and the orphan mindset attempts to pull you back into striving, fear, or self-protection. But now you know how to recognize the voice. And more importantly, you know it no longer has authority over your identity. You are no longer fighting for a seat at the table—you already have one.

Let the truth settle: You are chosen. You are adopted. You belong. Your name is on the seat, and the Father is smiling—waiting for you to take your place.

Reflection Questions

1. In what areas of your life are you still living like a spiritual orphan instead of a son or daughter? As you reflect, consider where fear, striving, insecurity, self-protection, or the need to prove yourself may still be shaping the way you think, respond, or connect with others.

2. What would it practically look like for you to fully embrace your seat at the Father's table? How would your relationships, decisions, confidence, and daily walk with God change if you truly believed you already belonged?

3. Which truth about sonship or daughter-ship do you need to begin declaring over yourself today? What truth from God's Word needs to become louder than the fear, rejection, or insecurity you've been carrying?

CHAPTER VII

From Rejected to Chosen

Chapter Seven

From Rejected to Chosen

If you've made it this far, then you've seen it. Not just on the surface, but deep down. You've seen how the orphan spirit works, how it hides in your thinking, how it shows up in your relationships, and how it shapes the way you see yourself and even the way you see God. You've started recognizing the patterns that once felt normal—the striving, fear, isolation, the constant pressure to prove yourself, protect yourself, or figure everything out on your own.

And maybe for the first time, you're beginning to realize that what you thought was just "your personality" or "the way you are" may have been wounds shaping your identity all along. Because the orphan mindset doesn't just influence behavior—it influences perspective. It changes how you receive love, how you respond to correction, and how safe you feel allowing people to truly know you.

And maybe, if you've been honest, you've seen yourself in it. Not in a way that brings shame, but in a way that brings clarity. Because this journey was never about pointing fingers.

It was about helping you recognize what's been operating in the background of your life, so you can finally be free from it.

And now we've come to the moment where everything shifts. Because at the end of all of this, it isn't just about what you've been through. It's about what God has done. This is where rejection meets redemption, where your past meets His grace, and where the lie you believed collides with the truth He's been speaking over you all along.

I did everything I could to get sent back. I pushed people away. I broke what others tried to build. I hurt the ones who tried to love me because I was already convinced, they would leave anyway. So, I beat them to it. I made it easy for them to walk away because deep down I believed one thing: "No one stays." But You did. You adopted me. You knew my story, saw my record, and understood the damage I had done. You knew how many bridges I burned and how many times I hardened my heart just to protect myself from being hurt again. You knew I would test Your love. You knew I would run, rage, and doubt. And still, You wanted me.

You weren't fostering me temporarily while waiting for someone better to come along. You didn't take me in with conditions, limitations, or hidden clauses. You adopted me— final, legal, eternal. When I felt like I was aging out emotionally, spiritually, and mentally, believing no one would come for me, You showed up. And what undoes me is knowing that You factored it all in. Every failure. Every relapse. Every moment I tried convincing You I wasn't worth loving. You saw all of it beforehand and still chose me anyway.

And this is where everything changes. Because the orphan spirit says, "You're too far gone," "You've messed up too much," and "You've pushed too many people away." But the Father never speaks like that. The orphan spirit condemns, shames, and reminds you of your failures, while the Father restores, covers, and calls you His own. He does not define you by the worst thing you've done or the moments you almost gave up. He defines you by His love, His grace, and the fact that He chose you before you ever learned how to choose Him back.

He doesn't look at your past and decide your value. He doesn't measure your worth by your worst moments, and He doesn't withdraw His love when you struggle to receive it. Instead, He steps in—not when you have it all together, not when you've proven yourself, and not when you finally get everything right, but right in the middle of your mess. Right in the middle of your doubt, your running, your resistance, and your fear. That's where He meets you.

And what makes this so powerful is knowing that He already knew. He knew how you would struggle. He knew where you would fall short and all the ways you would question Him along the journey. Yet none of it changed His mind. He didn't pull back, reconsider, or choose someone easier to love. He chose you. He saw every broken place, every failure, every hidden insecurity, and still decided you were worth pursuing.

You took the risk because You saw the reward, and the reward was me. You wanted me so deeply that You gave Your life in my place. You sealed my adoption not with ink, but with blood. You wrote me into Your family forever and gave me Your name. I'm not just forgiven and I'm not just accepted—I'm Yours.

I am not a burden You merely tolerate, and I'm not a mistake You regret. I am Your joy, Your delight, and Your great accomplishment. And maybe that's the hardest truth for the orphan mindset to accept: that the Father doesn't love you reluctantly. He loves you fully, intentionally, and without regret. Not because you earned it, but because love is who He is.

Reflection Questions

1. As you reflect on this chapter, where have you seen the orphan mindset operating most strongly in your life? How has it affected the way you receive love, respond to people, or view yourself and God?

2. Have there been moments where you pushed people away, sabotaged connection, or emotionally withdrew because deep down you expected rejection anyway? What belief was driving those reactions beneath the surface?

3. What part of the Father's love is hardest for you to truly receive—that He chose you, stays with you, fully knows you, or loves you without regret? Why do you think that truth feels difficult to embrace?

4. How would your life begin to change if you fully believed that God does not define you by your failures, your past, or your worst moments, but by His love and His decision to call you His own?

5. What would it look like for you to stop living from shame, fear, or survival and start living from the truth that you are fully adopted, fully accepted, and fully loved by the Father?

CHAPTER VIII

Now What?
Living as a Son, Walking as a
Daughter

Chapter Eight

Now What? Living as a Son or Daughter

At this point, you've probably realized something important: healing is not just about discovering what hurt you. It's about learning how to live differently because of what God is healing in you. Because once the orphan mindset is exposed, you can no longer pretend you don't see it. You begin noticing the patterns, the reactions, the thoughts, and the ways fear has quietly been influencing your life. And while that awareness can feel uncomfortable at first, it's also the beginning of freedom.

But freedom doesn't happen through information alone. It happens through intentional renewal. Through learning how to pause before reacting. Through recognizing when old thoughts are trying to pull you back into fear, striving, insecurity, or self-protection. Sonship is not just something you hear preached—it's something you practice daily. It's learning how to respond from identity instead of wounds.

And let's be honest, there will be moments when the old mindset tries to resurface. There will be days when insecurity speaks loudly, when rejection feels familiar, or when fear tempts you to pull away, shut down, or go back into survival mode. But healing is not about never struggling again. It's about no longer agreeing with the lies that once controlled you. It's about recognizing the voice of the orphan mindset and choosing not to partner with it anymore.

That's why this next section matters so much. Because these are not just "steps" or "tips." These are practical tools to help you renew your mind, strengthen your identity, and begin walking consistently as a son or daughter. Not perfectly, but intentionally. Because every time you choose truth over fear, connection over isolation, and trust over self-protection, you are teaching your mind and heart a new way to live.

You've seen it. You've recognized the patterns. You've felt the weight of it. And hopefully, you've also felt the invitation. So now the question becomes. What do you do with all of this? Because awareness is powerful…But transformation happens when you walk it out. This isn't about having a perfect day tomorrow. This is about deciding. I'm not going **back to thinking like an orphan.**

What This Looks Like in Real Life

Walking in sonship doesn't mean the thoughts stop overnight. It means you stop agreeing with them.

It means:

- When rejection tries to speak, you answer with truth

- When fear shows up, you don't let it lead

- When old patterns surface, you don't partner with them

You may still feel it…But you don't have to follow it.

This is a daily decision.

A Simple Daily Practice

Start here. Keep it simple. Stay consistent.

1. Check Your Thoughts

When something feels off, pause and ask:
"What am I believing right now?"

2. Challenge the Lie

Is it rooted in fear, rejection, or insecurity?
If it is, it's not the truth.

3. Replace It with Truth

Don't just reject the lie, replace it. Speak truth out loud.

4. Respond Differently

Choose a response that aligns with who you are becoming, not who you used to be.

Daily Declarations

Speak these every day out loud, with intention:

- I am not abandoned. I am chosen.

- I don't have to earn love—I live from it.

- I belong in every place God has called me to.

- I trust God's consistency, even when it feels unfamiliar.

- I am a son. I am a daughter. And I am secure.

Take It Deeper: Reflect and Be Honest

Don't rush this part. This is where real change begins.

Take time to journal.

- Where do I still think like an orphan?

- What situations trigger insecurity or fear in me?

- What lie have I believed for the longest time?

- What is God saying about me that I've struggled to accept?

- What would it look like to fully live like I belong?

Final Invitation

This is not a one-time moment—it's a new way of living. Healing, renewal, and walking in sonship or daughter-ship happen daily, one decision at a time. You don't have to do it perfectly, and you don't have to have every area figured out overnight. What matters is staying aware, staying honest, and staying willing to let God continue transforming the way you think and live.

Because every time you choose truth instead of fear, something shifts. Every time you choose to stay connected instead of running, every time you resist old patterns instead of partnering with them, and every time you remind yourself that you belong, you are breaking agreement with the orphan mindset.

Transformation happens in those moments. In the small daily choices to trust God when insecurity speaks, to receive love when fear tells you to pull away, and to rest in your identity instead of striving to earn it. And little by little, what once felt unfamiliar begins becoming your new normal.

And you are stepping into something deeper:

Life as a son.
Life as a daughter.
Life from a place of belonging.

Now walk in it.

About The Author

I am the son of Isiah and Andrea Williams, raised by a strong and faithful mother while my father was incarcerated for 26 years. Today, he's home, and by God's grace, my parents are still married. That alone is a testimony.

Now, I am a proud husband to Kelli Williams and a father to Taylor and Londyn—roles that continually remind me of the goodness, faithfulness, and redeeming power of God. My wife and I are the lead Pastors of Reach City Church, in the DFW area, in Texas.

My journey hasn't been without challenges, but through every season, God has been intentional in shaping my identity and calling. What once felt like absence, confusion, and uncertainty, He has redeemed with purpose, clarity, and direction.

The heart behind this message is simple: I want people to know they are sons and daughters. I want them to know they have a place. You don't have to live beneath labels, wounds, or identities that were placed on you by life or circumstances.

My prayer is that every reader would find the courage to confront the roots of their identity struggles and walk fully in the truth— that they were created in His image, fully seen, fully known, and fully loved.

Connect With Isiah Williams

Reach City Church
www.thereachcitychurch.com

Instagram: @ iamisiahwilliams
Facebook: Isiah Williams
YouTube: @ReachCity-Church

For speaking engagements or inquiries:
hello@reachcitychurch.org